Every Day

Paul's Prayers for the Church

© Waverley Abbey Resources 2021
Published 2021 by Waverley Abbey Resources. Waverley Abbey Resources
is a trading name of CWR, Waverley Abbey House, Waverley Lane, Farnham,
Surrey GU9 8EP, UK
Registered Charity No. 294387 Registered Limited Company No. 1990308

Unless otherwise indicated, all Scripture references are from The Holy Bible,
New International Version (Anglicised edition), copyright © 1979, 1984,
2011 by Biblica (formerly International Bible Society).

Concept development, editing, design and production by Waverley Abbey
Resources.
Front cover image: iStock
Printed in the UK by Yeomans

MIX
Paper from
responsible sources
FSC® C021017

WAVERLEY ABBEY
RESOURCES

Trading name of CWR

How to get the best out of
Life Every Day

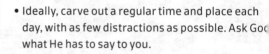

- Ideally, carve out a regular time and place each day, with as few distractions as possible. Ask God what He has to say to you.

- Read the Bible passages suggested in the 'Read' references. (As tempting as it is, try not to skip the Bible reading and get straight into the notes.)

- The 'FOCUS:' reference then gives you one or two verses to look at in more detail. Consider what the reading is saying to you and what challenges that may bring.

- Each day's comments are part of an overall theme. Try to recall what you read the previous day so that you maintain a sense of continuity.

- Spend time thinking about how to apply what God has said to you. Ask Him to help you do this.

- Pray the prayer at the end as if it were your own. Perhaps add your own prayer in response to what you have read and been thinking about.

Join in the conversation on Facebook
facebook.com/jefflucasuk

Paul's prayer for the Ephesians

Prayer often has a tame reputation. When people hear about it , they associate the practice with pleasant Sunday morning gatherings where nice people sing songs, read sacred texts and then have a cup of tea. Or prayer can be viewed broadly as something spiritual searchers do as an act of self-improvement, because they are in pursuit of personal enlightenment. But as we turn to this great prayer the apostle Paul prayed for his Christian friends in Ephesus, we will learn that prayer is a weapon. It is a mighty, powerful tool that we use as soldiers in the army of God, engaged as we are in the great war between good and evil, God's purposes and Satan's undermining strategies. We'll see that tussle being played out in Ephesus in the coming days – the gospel was preached with signs and wonders, but it was also heavily contested.

More tomorrow but for now, allow me to confess that I often forget the battle still rages. During the second World War, posters were displayed with the caption, 'Don't you know there's a war on?' Apparently as those terrible days of war rumbled on, people sometimes slipped into complacency, neglecting blackout laws, engaging in careless talk, and generally being less attentive and diligent. Something similar can happen to us. When life gets hard, temptation beckons, and we can be lured into settling for a benign, comfortable faith. We must remember we are living on the battlefield, where prayer is one of our most powerful weapons.

Read:
Ephesians 1:15–18
Ephesians 3:14–21

FOCUS:
'I have not stopped giving thanks for you, remembering you in my prayers.' (Eph. 1:16).

Prayer: Lord, please help to fight the good fight. Amen.

Don't get stuck

Read
Acts 19:1–7
Ephesians 3:14–21

FOCUS:

'Paul entered the synagogue and spoke boldly there for three months, arguing persuasively about the kingdom of God.'
(Acts 19:8)

Before we take a more detailed look at Paul's great prayer for the Ephesians, look at it with me again. Paul is praying for growth in his Christian friends there – strength, power, faith, stability, and an increasing ability to rest in and grasp the enormity of God's love for them – all signs of maturity.

We learn from Acts (which we'll look at for a few days) that the church in Ephesus, although blessed by the teaching of Apollos, had stalled. They needed further help to grow in their faith. The church there had grasped John the Baptist's call to repentance, but had not been taught about new life in Christ – hence their experience now of the Holy Spirit and their baptism in water in response to Paul's message. It was not their fault, but there was much more for them to learn.

New Christians tend to grow a lot to start with, hungry to understand the truths of their newfound faith. Tragically, after a while, having accumulated a certain amount of understanding and biblical wisdom, their appetite for growth can slow down or even splutter to a total halt. There is, however, so much to grasp about the infinite God we serve. We are not called to graduate this side of eternity, but to continue growing in our knowledge of God for the rest of our lives. And that's not just about accumulating more information, but applying God's word and living in His power each day. Are we still growing, or do we need the Lord to birth a fresh hunger for Him in our souls?

Prayer: Stir me, Lord. Unsettle me, birth in me hunger pangs for You. Amen.

Are we still growing...?

I'll pray about it

Read
Acts 19:8–12
1 Corinthians
15:1–11

As a young pastor, I got the same response every time I approached a particular gentleman to ask him to help and serve. We were a small, busy church, and we needed everyone on board to fulfil our mission. The chap in question was very vocal about all that we should be doing, and very critical about what he saw as gaps in our approach, but whenever I asked him to roll up his sleeves and get involved, I got the same response: 'I'm praying about it.' It suggested his passivity was simply that he wanted to ensure he only responded to God's calling. But it is clear that Paul prayed for *and* worked hard in Ephesus. Spending around three years serving there, and being tenacious and adaptable in the face of opposition (first using the synagogue to debate, and then a local lecture hall), he worked tirelessly. He provided his own income from his leather work, served and prayed. Let's follow his example. And if we feel disinclined to serve, let's not hide our inactivity behind pious language.

To ponder: Is prayer and service balanced in your life?

Spiritual warfare

Read
Acts 19:13–16
1 Peter 5:8–11

FOCUS:

'Then the man who had the evil spirit jumped on them and overpowered them all. He gave them such a beating that they ran out of the house naked and bleeding.'
(Acts 19:16)

Talking recently with a fine local church leader who has just been the victim of a clear conspiracy by others who wanted his position, he was in tears as he described the awful experience of being betrayed by those he had considered to be friends and colleagues. Tracing his journey, however, he was able to look past the human players in the drama. 'I've battled principalities and powers these last months' he said. 'Satan has fought my family and me in a way we've never experienced before.' His comments suddenly alerted me to a truth that I mentioned earlier –we are in a spiritual war. Just a brief glance at all that unfolded in the city of Ephesus reminds us of that very clearly. Demonic spirits infested the culture there. Paganism and sorcery were rife. The brutal encounter with the evil spirit in Acts 19 shows that Ephesus really was a battleground, and the forces of darkness don't give up territory without a fight.

The powers of darkness are real, but also subtle. It's been said that the devil's shoes don't creak. Why not take some time to consider where we might be falling into some deception that is not just rooted in ignorance but is a result of the work of the enemy of our souls? Even as I write these words, I know that they seem primitive – but as we affirm the reality of goodness and God, so we know that there is such a personality as the prince of evil. He is on the prowl. While we don't need to be paranoid, we do need to be diligent.

Prayer: Open my eyes to the reality of the warfare that rages, Lord, and protect my heart as I continue my journey. Amen.

The Big Bounce Forwards

The Big Church Read

Bouncing Forwards by Patrick Regan has been chosen for the Big Church Read. Here's what you need to know. The Big Church read is all about journeying through the book with the author, and then meeting in-person or online to talk about what they have read.

After a tough year for the Church, Waverley Abbey Resources are proud to be supporting this fantastic initiative, and we're so pleased that *Bouncing Forwards* has been selected for it. From 8 September, each Wednesday morning for 10 weeks the Big Church Read will release weekly exclusive videos and content from Patrick Regan to enhance your reading experience.

About Bouncing Forwards

We've all faced difficulties over the last year in some shape or form. Often when we go through challenging times, we're told, 'You'll bounce back.' As well-meant as these words area, the tough times we've been through leave us scarred and changed – so why would we want to go back when we've learnt so much? It's time to bounce *forwards* instead.

In *Bouncing Forwards*, Patrick draws on his own journey of making peace with his on-going anxiety, to look honestly and vulnerably at the temptation to wait for the day when all will be well whilst missing out on what's happening in the here and now. Exploring resilience, acceptance and emotional agility, Patrick shows how we can find meaning in some of life's toughest moments and the hope to journey on.

To find out more about Bouncing Forwards and the Big Church Read, and to make use of the **bulk-buy discount**, visit **waverleyabbeyresources.org/bf**

Costly faith

Read:
Acts 19: 17– 41
Ephesians 5:11

....

FOCUS:

'A number who had practised sorcery brought their scrolls together and burned them publicly.'
(Acts 19:19)

As Christians living in a country where being a follower of Jesus is acceptable and often even respectable, our faith can cost us little. Unlike our brothers and sisters in the persecuted church around the world, we can therefore settle into comfortable complacency, where faith places little demand on our day-to-day living. Faith becomes something to comfort us when life is tough, but it's not valuable enough to nudge us to costly commitment, never mind endurance in persecution.

In Ephesus, in the maelstrom of spiritual warfare that we've been discussing, the new believers there immediately demonstrated their commitment to Jesus in the way they rejected their former lifestyle, which had been steeped in the occult. These scrolls that went into the fire were extremely valuable; they might have rationalised that, while they needed to get rid of them, they could have sold them and realised the income. But they made a clear stand, one that had a further great effect on that dark city. Their commitment was so impressive, it triggered a response from others as the 'word of the Lord spread widely and grew in power'. We learn that the occult is not something to be played with (not because there's nothing in it, but as the story of the demon-possessed man proves, there's something very dark in it), but we also see being disciples of Jesus will at times be very costly. When the opportunity comes to sacrifice because of obedience, may we be found faithful.

Prayer: When faith moves beyond comfort to cost, enable me to live in a way that glorifies Your Name, Father. Amen

Faith in God, love for God's people

As we begin to look at the first part of Paul's prayer for the Ephesians, we should consider the news he's heard about them: the good news about their faith in Christ and their love for all God's people. The two should go hand in hand, our relationship with the Lord profoundly affecting the way we are with others, showing them love. It should be obvious that both are vital, and in his epistle, John makes it clear that the one who says they love God and hates others is a liar. But in my experience (and sadly, at times in my own life) I have tried to separate these two virtues, wanting to love and serve God, but holding on to bitterness towards those who have bruised me. Others show little love for God's people, simply because they have chosen to walk the Christian pathway alone. Rejecting church as outmoded, and focusing on the hurts they've experienced, they withdraw from meaningful church relationships. One of the main truths that emerges from Paul's letter to the Ephesians is God has created a people, not just persons, for Himself. Solitary Christianity doesn't work and is theologically untenable. If your local church has wounded you, I'm sorry, but I pray you will not allow your negative experience to drive you into the wilderness of being alone. If trust has been damaged by abusive leadership, find someone to share with and aim to move forward in healthy fellowship. Painful though it can be at times, we belong together, as God's loving people.

Prayer: I am loved by You, and I love You, Lord. Enable me to love others, especially those who challenge me the most. Amen.

Read:
Ephesians 1:1–16
1 John 2:3–11

FOCUS:
'For this reason, ever since I heard about your faith in the Lord Jesus and your love for all God's people, I have not stopped giving thanks for you.' (Eph. 1:15–16)

we belong
together

Wisdom and revelation

Read:
Ephesians 1:17
Philippians 3:1–14

....

FOCUS:

'I keep asking that the God of our Lord Jesus Christ, the glorious Father, may give you the Spirit of wisdom and revelation, so that you may know him better.' (Eph. 1:17)

Regular readers of *Life Every Day* will know that I spend some of my life as a coach and facilitator using the LifePlan process. We spend a lot of time considering and charting the client's life journey to date. We create a large storyboard that maps out their life experience, and consider the key junctions that they've navigated. The purpose of this is to glean wisdom from their pathway. Christians can emphasise revelation – God speaking – but fail to prize wisdom – lessons we learn, both from Scripture and experience, that we can apply to our lives now. In his prayer for the Ephesians, Paul asks for wisdom as well as revelation, but also points to the God who works by His Spirit to help us experience both. But this is more than just careful reflection and self-discovery. Both wisdom and revelation are linked with knowing God more and more, or to quote Paul exactly, knowing Him 'better'. Growing deeper in his relationship with the Lord was Paul's greatest and primary ambition, as his words to the Philippians show. Learning to hear God's voice, sensing His direction, submitting to those nudges from His Spirit all are part of what it means to walk with God.

Perhaps, like me, you find these words deeply challenging. Our priorities can stifle our call to know and walk with God by faith. As we determine each day to talk with Him, be open to His voice, immerse our hearts and minds in Scripture, then wisdom and revelation will result.

Prayer: Place in me a hunger for greater knowledge of You, Lord Jesus. In knowing You, there is wisdom. Amen

A heart with eyes on hope

Read:
Ephesians 1:17–19
2 Peter 3:1–18

FOCUS:
'I pray that the eyes of your heart may be enlightened in order that you may know the hope to which he has called you.' (Eph. 1: 18)

Hoping can sound like wishing. As I write this, I hope that the wildfires in Colorado will be finally quenched, an effective vaccine will beat the dreaded Covid, and the relentless rain currently drenching England will stop and make way for a little sunshine (yes, I write these notes months ahead of time). The word 'hope' seems tentative, meaning we can see something is possible, yet realise it is by no means certain. But Christian hope is not at all like that. Our hope in Jesus is sure and certain, because Christ has died, Christ is risen, and Christ will come again.

Over the years, I've been reluctant to speak about eschatology (the study of the End Times) because so much speculation and silliness had surrounded the subject. So-called 'prophets' have made ridiculous and unbiblical predictions, and books sold by the millions outlining what is supposedly coming. And when they have turned out to be false, new ones have replaced them. Preachers have distorted the meaning of Bible books such as Daniel and Revelation, and tried to turn them into calendars, which is not their purpose.

Despite all that, our hope is this: God has not abandoned the world, and His purposes will come to pass. Ultimately, the death, resurrection and ascension of Jesus has rendered even death powerless, the 'last enemy' of humanity. May we have 'enlightened eyes in our hearts' to see that which is only visible by faith, but is eternally secure – our hope in Jesus Christ.

Prayer: In You, Lord Jesus, my hope is found, firm, secure, certain. I declare it. Amen.

Our hope in Jesus is sure and certain

Read:
Ephesians 1:18
Colossians 1:9–12

Being together – a priceless privilege

Reviewing an ongoing online argument between some very loud and opinionated Christians, I almost despaired. For just a moment, I wanted to have nothing more to do with the Church. From the moment of my conversion, I have loved the Church. As a lonely and bewildered teenager, I was welcomed with open arms and relentless kindness by a small but passionate congregation, and I have spent my life and ministry teaching, preaching and writing with a specific burden to encourage the local church. Once in a while, however, I feel overwhelmed by the petty bickering that can characterise the Church. But as we read words from Paul's prayer where he celebrates 'the riches of his glorious inheritance in his holy people', we're reminded that while fellowship can be painful, it is priceless.

Commentators believe Paul is celebrating the truth that in Jesus, we belong, we take our place among the people of God. Those who cause us grief are nevertheless part of a holy people set apart for God's purposes.

To ponder: For you, what is the greatest blessing, and what is the greatest challenge that come from being part of God's Church?

Visit **waverleyabbey resources.org /podcast** to listen to a podcast

od's power is available to us. His power is
mighty. God is all powerful. The God who created
erything with a word – His power is in us and for us.
I know, you're thinking the above sentences do not
nstitute the best writing I've produced – but this is
actly the approach that Paul employs. As he stresses
d celebrates God's power to the Ephesians, he
acks up four words for power in order to convey the
ightiness of God. Why? Perhaps it's because we can
nd to think of God's incredible power as something
ostract, just a doctrine we subscribe to, and forget
at it is available to work in us and through us – notice
ul's phrase, 'for us who believe'. Christianity is not
oout fragile humans doing our best to do what's right
people of faith; rather, it's about us cooperating
th the mighty God who energises us and empowers
to live beautifully for His glory.

To further hammer the wonderful point home, Paul
oints us to a graphic example of that power, God's
oility to raise a three-day dead body to life in the
ising of Jesus. And Paul will return to the power
eme once again when he draws his letter to a close,
lling the Ephesians to 'be strong in the Lord and in
s mighty power' (Eph. 6:10).

Perhaps you feel weak today, unable to be resolute
th all of the challenges that you face. Help is at hand,
d power is available. May you be strengthened with
at power in the battles that you face.

ayer: Fill me afresh with power from on high this day,
ghty God. Amen.

Power available

Read:
Ephesians 1:18–19
Colossians 1:29

FOCUS:

'And his incomparably great power for us who believe.' (Eph. 1:19)

A glorious distraction

Read:
Ephesians 2:1–22
Hebrews 12:1–2

....

FOCUS:

'All of us also lived among them at one time, gratifying the cravings of our flesh and following its desires and thoughts. Like the rest, we were by nature deserving of wrath.' (Eph. 2:3)

I often say that praying is difficult. Talking to someone who is currently invisible has its challenges. Many preachers teach prayer is a conversation (I've taught it myself in the past), but the reality is, at least for me, most of the time it is nothing like a conversation. Even though there are times when I do feel a nudge or a hint, or hear a whisper of His voice, it still doesn't feel like a clear conversation. All of these challenges mean I often get distracted when I pray, and my mind wanders off to something less important.

In this two-part prayer, Paul also got distracted, and broke off his praying midway – we'll pick it up again tomorrow when we consider chapter 3. But I am challenged by the content of Paul's distraction. He meanders into glorious reflections about grace, God's love and inclusion of all people, and then considers his own calling to serve that amazing Jesus. I'd love to be able to say I am distracted *by* Jesus, rather than the truth being that I am distracted *from* Him by the pressures and concerns of everyday life. Perhaps Paul's distraction was caused by his knowledge that, despite his appalling crimes against Christ and His church prior to his conversion, the God of grace had found him and was keeping him. Today, look back, and recall the goodness of God to you. Fill your mind and heart with worship and praise as you do so. As we 'fix our eyes' on Christ by faith, we'll surely be strengthened for the journey we take today.

recall the goodness of God to you

Prayer: Help me to fix my eyes on You by faith, especially when fear, temptation or just the humdrum of life threatens to take my focus. Amen.

he God to whom we pray

e talked about it before in *Life Every Day*, but as I
ead of Paul bowing before the Father (an unusual
rm, as the ancient practice was to stand while
aying, so this might suggest a special earnestness),
n reminded of speaking at a Christian event, many
ars ago. 'Solid Ground' was a youth event, held on
very wet, muddy field, and I was due to speak about
e power of the Holy Spirit. The idea of power can
 intimidating, so I held my then two-year-old son
 my arms as I began to preach, illustrating the truth
at healthy fatherhood brings security. Suddenly he
rew open his arms and buried his head into my neck.
 that moment, it was like a thunderclap of power
t that gathering, in what was, without question,
e most amazing service that I've been to in four
cades. All these years later I still meet people who
 member that night when many were healed, saved
d delivered – and it happened as a simple portrait of
therhood was demonstrated.

In using language that's difficult to fully understand,
ul points to the Father after whom every family in
aven and earth' has been named and derived, the
ther who is not just good, but unlike any other father.
sus echoes this teaching as He instructs us to begin
r prayers with the words 'Our Father'.

The key to a healthy life of prayer, and indeed to all
 life itself, is the knowledge that we have a Father
ho loves and cares for us superlatively. Me. You.
ght now.

ayer: Not only am I blessed to call You Father, but in
u, I am safe and secure. Amen.

Read:
Ephesians 3:14–15
Matthew 6:9–13

FOCUS:
*'For this reason I
kneel before the
Father, from whom
every family in
heaven and on earth
derives its name.'
(Eph. 3:14–15)*

There's good within us

Read:
Ephesians 3:16–17
Luke 4:1–13

FOCUS:

'I pray that out of his glorious riches he may strengthen you with power through his Spirit... so that Christ may dwell in your hearts through faith.' (Eph. 3:16–17)

I t happened again yesterday – a power cut. The lights went off, the freezer shut down, and frustration was the result. It seems that workmen had cut the line that led to the source, and until it is reconnected, there's nothing we can do. We cannot fix it; we cannot change it. We can feel the same way about problems and temptations in our own lives. We think we are powerless. But as Paul prays that his readers will know the power of God at work within them, we're reminded that we have a source available to enable us to make the right, healthy choices, when temptation comes. I am not talking about simple moral fortitude. What we are talking about here is God's power: urging, calling and even enabling us to resist what seems so enticing. The Holy Spirit within us not only quietly shapes and transforms us daily, but can empower us when we feel weak. This is a strength from beyond ourselves, coming straight from God Himself.

We are not at the mercy of temptation, no matter how strong the pull of compulsive and habitual behaviour might be. Temptation can make us feel both vulnerable and very alone. But just as Jesus went into the wilderness of temptation filled with the power of the Holy Spirit, so can we. Perhaps you're feeling as though you are very much in the grip of a destructive behaviour pattern in your life right now. A word from me won't fix that. But I do want you to know, based on all that Scripture says, that you are neither alone nor powerless.

The Holy Spirit... can empower us

Prayer: Empower me, fill me, bring good fruit into my life. I will work with You, Mighty Holy Spirit. Amen.

God settling in

'Ask Jesus to come into your heart.' It's a phrase that Christians often use when they share the good news of the gospel, and invite people to respond. Although the language might seem a little strange to outsiders, it's a biblical concept. Paul talks to the Romans about Christ being in them, (Rom. 8:10), living within the centre of their beings, as they and we are the temples of the Holy Spirit. And we saw yesterday that the power of the Holy Spirit is available to work within us with power. But why does Paul pray that Christ will dwell in the Ephesian's hearts by faith, because surely, they are Christians who have already made that decision? Paul's specific words shed some helpful light here. Apparently, there are two words that he uses to describe dwelling; one is the person who is temporarily away from home, and staying in overnight accommodation elsewhere before leaving for home the next day. The other portrays someone who makes their permanent home in a new location; they move in and settle there for good. That is the word Paul uses here, picturing a God who makes His home forever within the centre of our beings, ruling and reigning in our lives from there.

That's a beautiful portrait of the Christian life – not a compartmentalised one where church happens on Sunday and we then go off and live a contrary life on Monday, but a consistent, steady walk of discipleship through the minutes and the days, as we abide in Him and He abides in us.

Prayer: Abide with me, and know my consistent welcome to You in all areas of my life, at all times, Lord. Amen.

Read:
Ephesians 3:16–17
John 15:1–17

FOCUS:

'so that Christ may dwell in your hearts through faith.'
(Eph. 3:17)

Rooted and grounded

My recent attempt to plant a large jasmine bush resulted in blisters, and the chalky soil made it harder. The task required a spade, a pickaxe and a lot of muttering. Four hours later, the bush was planted. I thoroughly drenched the transplanted roots, obviously the source of life for the relocated bush, which is now doing well. It helped me to grasp the metaphors Paul uses here, drawing on both botany and building, as he prays the Ephesians will be 'rooted and established', planted and with secure foundations – in love. Paul then produces a torrent of superlatives about the love of God, describing indescribable dimensions and praying for knowledge of this love that's beyond knowing. We are loved with a love beyond our comprehension.

How often we forget what God not only feels for us, but how He acts towards us, even sending His own Son for our rescue. Whatever you are experiencing today in your circumstances, know this: God loves you a trillion times more than you realise. And then some.

To ponder: Is it easier to believe that God loves the world than it is to be assured He loves each one of us, individually and personally? If so, why?

a love beyond our comprehension.

We belong together

Years ago, I had the opportunity to work backstage in a small London theatre. It was all rather exciting, being up in the fly gallery, operating ropes and pulleys that enabled scenery changes, following the script to make sure that the relevant props were on hand. But seeing backstage meant that eventually the drama of the play was lost on me.

Sometimes I feel like that about the Church. I've been privileged to speak in over a thousand different local churches and conferences, and I've seen leaders, churches and Christians at their best – and, sadly, at their worst. Today I listened to a well-known speaker online, waxing eloquently about the power of love and healthy relationships. Sadly, I know the behind-the-scenes truth; he has a consistent reputation for being harsh with his team, cold and arrogant. And that 'backstage' knowledge can be disabling; for just a moment (or three), I felt again as though I wanted to have nothing more to do with the Church. But it's so clear from Scripture, as we have seen, that solitary Christianity is a misnomer. God's mission is to create a people in the earth, not just to rescue individuals and then leave them in isolation. As Paul prays the Ephesians will grasp something of the vastness of God's love, he reminds them they do this, 'together with all the Lord's holy people'. Fellowship can be frustrating and costly, but if we want to comprehend more of God and His love, we must do so together in community.

Prayer: When fellowship is more painful that pleasurable, help me to remember what I am part of – your holy people, Lord. Amen.

Read:
Ephesians 3:17–18
Ephesians 1:15–16

FOCUS:

'And I pray that you, being rooted and established in love, may have power, together with all the Lord's holy people.'
(Eph. 3:17–18)

The fulness of God

Read:
Ephesians 3:14–19
Romans 12:1–2

FOCUS:

'that you may be filled to the measure of all the fullness of God.' (Eph. 3:19)

It's a sad statement, one that I have made before, but it needs repeating: after over four decades of pastoral ministry, I've concluded that most people don't change that much. That sounds stark, and contradicts all we say we believe about the gospel. Surely it is the news of rebirth and ongoing transformation, a result of the work of the Spirit within us, as we have seen. So it's lamentable that, after a first flush of change in the early years after conversion, the temptation is to settle down and surrender into sameness. We can stop believing anything can be different; we are what we are.

Paul makes what one commentator*describes as an 'audacious' statement about our being filled with the fulness of God. It is a difficult phrase to grapple with, but probably means the character of God is gradually poured into us. Obviously, it's not that we become gods, but we become God-like, or godly. Ultimately, that process of change will not be completed until we finally meet Christ face to face, when we shall be like Him, sin and brokenness banished forever. But in the meantime, as we walk with Him as citizens of the kingdom that is now but not yet, being established in our lives but not yet full established on the earth, we must embrace not the vague possibility of change, but the expectation of it. For people being filled with God, change us not just possible, but inevitable.

Prayer: Save me from ever surrounding to sameness, Lord. Where I struggle to change, grant me hope and faith. Amen.

*Andrew T Lincoln, Word Bible Commentary, Ephesians, vol 42.

Beyond our imagining

As we come to the end of Paul's prayer in Ephesians 3, we can see again that he uses superlative after superlative to try to capture something of the stunning, jaw-dropping, unique nature of God; His power, His love, His glory. It's as if Paul is trying to somehow capture a fragment of the essence of the greatness of our God. In the end, it's impossible, and so he caps his prayer with words of praise that tell us however great we can imagine God to be, He is way beyond our imagining.

Again, I am writing these notes while the Covid pandemic still rages, the virus that has caused so much pain, disruption and death globally. It reminds our belief that we had everything under control was a myth. But the pandemic can also shrink our vision of God. We can feel a sense of universal importunity; many prayers have been prayed, but as yet there is no respite. That's why I want us to pause today and remember the truth that is unchanging, regardless of our circumstances or emotions. God is still bigger than anything we might face, and although I write these words with a mingled sense of joy and frustration, compared with God, nothing is an issue.

God is not, however, a genie in a bottle, ready to fulfil our wildest dreams. He is the Mighty One who invites us to participate in His kingdom dream. God is the One who spoke and brought the universe into being; at work in us and through His church. Let's never allow our vision of Him and His power to shrink.

Prayer: Rise up, Mighty God. Show Your power and glory, afresh in my world, afresh in me. Amen.

Read:
Ephesians 3:20–21
Genesis 1:1–31

FOCUS:
'Now to him who is able to do immeasurably more than all we ask or imagine, according to his power that is at work within us, to him be glory.'
(Eph. 3:20–21)

God is still bigger than anything we might face

And so to Philippi

Read:
Philippians 3:15–21
Ephesians 2:19

FOCUS:

'But our citizenship is in heaven.'
(Phil. 3:20)

We turn now to Paul's prayer for his friends in the city of Philippi. As we did with the prayer in the letter to the Ephesians, we'll spend a few days considering the context for Paul's prayer, his relationship with the people in that city, and the situation in which they found themselves. Events in recent years have generated quite a lot of shouting, with a pandemic and political uncertainties. At times like this, I think it's important to remember that as followers of Jesus, we all have dual citizenship. We are, *first and foremost*, citizens of the kingdom of God, and then *secondarily*, we carry whatever national citizenship we hold. But the kingdom comes first. There is more than life in the here and now.

Philippi was a proud, prosperous Roman colony. The lay-out of the city and its architecture were modelled on Rome, as were legal and administrative details in the way it was governed. The citizens wore Roman dress, had coinage with Roman inscriptions, and used (though not exclusively) the Latin language. It was also a prosperous place to live, being something of a resort town – the area was attractive because of the many springs in the vicinity, and the nearby gold mines. But Paul wanted the Philippians to know the importance of heavenly citizenship. Some Christians today also put their political allegiance before the kingdom. Let's remember that our primary identity is not as members of an earthly nation, but as members of His kingdom.

Prayer: My allegiance first and foremost is to You as a kingdom citizen, Lord. Help me to live in the fulness, privilege and responsibility of that identity. Amen.

COLLEGE   RESOURCES   HOUSE

rleyabbeycollege.ac.uk   waverleyabbeyresources.org   waverleyabbeyhouse.org

Waverley Abbey Trust

We are a charity serving Christians around the world with practical resources and teaching. We support you to grow in your Christian faith, understand the times in which we live, and serve God in every sphere of life.

The three main areas we focus on are:

- **Mental Health and Wellbeing**

- **Leadership**

- **Spiritual Formation**

waverleyabbey.org

The wall can be a door

Read:
Acts 16:6–8
Acts 14:27

FOCUS:

'When they came to the border of Mysia, they tried to enter Bithynia, but the Spirit of Jesus would not allow them to.'
(Acts 16:7)

Over four decades ago, Kay and I were presented with an amazing opportunity for ministry. The challenge was great, the potential influence for the gospel was incredible, and we felt enthusiastic and humbled to be invited to consider it. But then, through circumstances too convoluted to explain, we felt a strong check about moving forward. We declined the invitation, and went instead to what seemed to be an obscure and limited ministry situation. And I'm so very glad that we did. As we look back, we can see how God was both leading us and training us. What seemed like a wall, an obstacle to progress, turned out to be a doorway to all that God had in store.

In Acts, we discover the church in Philippi was birthed because Paul came up against a closed door. First planning to preach in Asia, we are told the Holy Spirit prevented him. Then, as Paul plans to visit Bithynia, we read that 'the Spirit of Jesus would not allow him to'. We see immediately how much Jesus is involved in the details of the great kingdom mission – more of that tomorrow. We're not told how this preventative move happened – some say it might have come through a prophetic utterance, perhaps through Silas, who was a prophet (Acts 15:32). Perhaps the team just shared an intuitive sense that this was God's direction, or circumstances such as illness or opposition stopped them. But for Paul, a wall became door to Ephesus. And the same can be true for us.

Prayer: Guide me, Lord, and give me confidence that when a door shuts, You are working out Your plans for me. Amen.

A call – we are on God's mission

'Your mission, should you choose to accept it…' So begins the opening sequence of the Mission Impossible movie, with Tom Cruise embracing the role of tenacious hero. We too, are called to live heroically, sacrificing where needed for the mission of the gospel. But as we read yesterday about the Holy Spirit intervening in Paul's plans, stopping him heading in one direction and opening a door for another avenue of ministry, we're reminded that the mission is God's, not ours. We are invited to partner with Him, but we are very much junior partners. We are not there to drive forward our own good ideas and initiatives, but to submit our plans to the One who owns the planet and owns the Church. We are participants in the *Missio Dei* the mission of God. And the same is true of our lives. We are not our own, we've been bought with a price. Having given our lives to Jesus, let's not gradually take them back again, but commit ourselves afresh to live for His priorities and purposes.

To ponder: Have you ever been a victim of your own 'good' idea, because you mistakenly thought it was God's idea?

Weekend

Your mission, should you choose to accept it…'

Thoughtful, shared spirituality

FOCUS:

'After Paul had seen the vision, we got ready at once to leave for Macedonia, concluding that God had called us to preach the gospel to them.' (Acts 16:10)

Surely it happens countless times every day, as Christians boldly announce, 'God told me.' And God is not mute, He does speak and guide. But through the years, I have heard too many declarations that God has decreed something, only to find the initiative His 'speaking' launched came to nothing, or a prediction did not come to pass. We've already seen doors had closed for Paul and his team, but God did not leave them without direction and strategy. Paul has a dream which includes a call from a man from Macedonia. It's worth noting it includes a plea for 'help' – the Christian message is the most 'helpful' news in the Universe. When we share it, we enable other human beings to live the way that the Creator always intended.

As we read that Paul's team 'concluded' God was indeed the author of the dream, we come across a word Paul used that speaks of shared discussion, the group being ultimately convinced. Evidently Paul did not just say, 'I've had a dream, let's go.' He brought what he sensed he was hearing from God into a context for evaluation. Something similar happened in Jerusalem as the church there conclude, 'It seemed good to the Holy Spirit and to us.'

Paul and his team concluded God was leading them to Europe, and once consensus was found, they began their missionary journey at once. When we feel God has spoken, a mature response would be for us to do the same, and follow up a shared decision.

Prayer: Thank You, Father, for the gift of shared counsel. Help me to build relationships where I can find safety, confirmation and challenge. Amen.

Praying in jail

The hideous scourge of human trafficking around the world – and in our own communities – has been highlighted in recent years, and organisations such as Stop the Traffik are working hard to combat it. It is nothing new, however. Paul and Silas are arrested because some traffickers are angry that their 'commodity', a slave girl, has lost a demon – and her gift of clairvoyance with it. Because she is no longer useful to them, they are furious, but they disguise their rage at losing money by trumping up a charge about the missionary pair being 'anti-Roman', which leads to a very severe beating and overnight imprisonment.

In the midst of all this pain, Paul and Silas sing, in the middle of the night. I've always thought they worshipped because they were unafraid, but perhaps that's wrong. Is it possible they sang *because* they were afraid, and the joining of their voices together galvanised them for whatever lay ahead? When we consider Paul's sufferings and the weakness he describes in his letters, it becomes clear he was not superhuman. At times, he wrestled with despair. But surely worship helped him put his trust in Christ. That is what happens to me when I stand with the family of God: I worship because life is so uncertain, not because it isn't. As I worship, as a statement of truth, not of my mood, I am strengthened. Perhaps we should sing more about who God is, rather than about how we feel. Our emotions and circumstances change. He does not.

Prayer: Faithful God, for the gift of togetherness and fellowship, especially when clouds gather, I am grateful. Amen.

Read:
Acts 16:19–40
Psalm 56:1–4

FOCUS:

'About midnight Paul and Silas were praying and singing hymns to God, and the other prisoners were listening to them.' (Acts 16:25)

Perhaps we should sing more about who God is

Paul the politician

Read:
Acts 16:16–40
Micah 6:8

FOCUS:

"They beat us publicly without a trial, even though we are Roman citizens, and threw us into prison. And now do they want to get rid of us quietly? No!"
(Acts 16:37)

It was a divinely orchestrated jailbreak, as the ground trembles with an earthquake, cell doors fly open, a jailor is about to commit suicide, and then he and his family become converts. Now the local magistrates want to be rid of Paul and Silas as quickly as possible. But Paul (and Silas) refuse to budge. Both of them are Roman citizens, and their rights have been totally violated because they were both beaten and imprisoned – a very serious breach of the law. And so rather than scurrying off to freedom, he insists the local authorities come and escort them out of prison. So why did Paul insist on the apology from the local civic leaders?

Commentators are uncertain, but some suggest he did this to prove publicly that, in sharing the gospel, he had done nothing illegal. That vindication would be vital for the local believers he will leave behind as he ultimately leaves the city. This is a wise and politically shrewd move, and it also shows Paul not only prays for the Christian community in Philippi, but he uses his rights to their advantage too. Those who believe we should not use our voices to influence the political arena are surely wrong; we pray, we act. In studying the prayers of Paul, we should not forget that he also took other steps to serve and bless. We are not called to retreat from the world, using our prayer for it as an excuse for inaction; God wants us to do good in the world; to pray, speak, act, give, and serve to the best of our ability.

Prayer: Father, as opportunity and need arise, help me to make a difference in my world as I live, pray, speak and work for You. Amen.

Depth of love

Attending a conference for pastors, I was keen to learn from men and women who had proven track records in leadership. Hurrying to a session led by a man who had taken a tiny church to one of multiple thousands meeting in many campuses, I was hopeful he might share some nuggets of wisdom. But I was disappointed. He spoke endlessly about programmes, techniques, marketing and structures, but when asked about caring for people, his response surprised us. 'I don't really like people, to be honest. I try to avoid them and leave all that to others on my staff.' While I recognise that we all have different temperaments and gifts, surely loving people has to be the foundation for Christian ministry. God loves His world and all in it – if we don't love people, our motives for serving must be suspect.

As Paul greets the believers in Philippi, he uses language of deep affection – they were among his favourites, and had shown genuine care for him in the support of his ministry. As he says, 'God can testify', he effectively makes an oath: 'God knows how much I love you.' Later in his letter, he writes of them as 'you whom I love and long for, my joy and crown'. This is a man with more than message – he deeply, passionately cares for the believers he had reached and nurtured in his repeated visits. We're not all 'people' people – some of us prefer our own company to the crowd. But regardless of our temperament, we are all called to treat people with love.

Prayer: Today, may I love others, not only in word but in deed, in humility, in serving, in prayer. Amen.

Read:
Philippians 1:1–8
Philippians 4:1

FOCUS:

'God can testify how I long for all of you with the affection of Christ Jesus.'
(Phil. 1:8).

we are all called to treat people with love.

A friend like Paul

Read:
Philippians 1:1–11
2 Corinthians 7:3

FOCUS:

'It is right for me to feel this way about all of you, since I have you in my heart and ... all of you share in God's grace with me.'
(Phil. 1:7)

Friends – we all want them, and hopefully we all want to be better at the art of friendship. If that's to be true, we need to be intentional and invest in friendships. Years ago, Roger Forster commented that we need more than friendships, we need kingdom relationships. The apostle Paul, as a true friend to the Christian community in Philippi, exemplifies what it means to be a good, kingdom friend. The foundations of a kingdom friendship are found in Philippians chapte 1. Paul was able to honestly say that he has them in his mind, 'I remember you' (Phil. 1:3). He thought about them, considered their challenges, pondered what they needed. Then he affirmed, 'I have you in my heart' (Phil. 1:7–8).His was more than a passing interest: he showed deep, heartfelt care, as we saw yesterday. And then, he regularly and consistently brought them befor the Lord: 'this is my prayer' (Phil. 1:9–11). I think all thre elements are important; it's only as we reflect upon other's lives that we can pray intelligently, and we'll only do that consistently when we genuinely care for them.

In the kingdom, we're to build friendships that go beyond times of fun and shared interests, although those are important. We need to have friends, and to be thoughtful, loving and prayerful friends. We need friendships that inspire us and others to excellence, commitment and faithfulness to Jesus. I have some friends just like that, and having them in my life make me rich.

Prayer: I'm thankful for friendships of depth, substance and spiritual strength. Help me to be that kind of friend, Father. Amen.

Read:
Philippians 4:4–9
Philippians 3:1

A people under pressure

et's look at the situation the Philippians were in when
'aul sent them this letter, around ten years after his
irst visit. They were under serious pressure. They
vere worried about Paul's imprisonment – he had
lready served a two-year stretch (Acts 24:27). There
vas an increasing sense of the depravity of the culture
hey lived in, hence Paul's call to them to live as bright
ghts. Paul gives an update on one of their leaders,
paphroditus, who had been sent from Philippi to
isit Paul in prison. He had nearly died. False teachers
vere trying to infiltrate the church (chapter 3), and
ivision, hinted at throughout the letter but addressed
xplicitly in chapter 4, was a worrying threat. They are
roubled. This letter is known as the epistle of joy, but
aul's repeated exhortations indicate their lack of joy.
s I have often said, following Jesus is not a guarantee
f a pressure-free life. Being known as His people
night multiply our troubles. When it does, may we
earn to rejoice.

o ponder: What does it mean to rejoice?

Visit the Holy Land and Jordan
9-17th November 2021

Join Jeff and Kay Lucas on a life changing tour of Israel and Jordan, visiting famous sites that will transform the way you read and view the Bible, including Galilee, Jerusalem and Magdala, the home of Mary Magdalene. Capernaum and the Garden of Gethsemane are included, as well as the amazing desert landscape of Wadi Rum with its idyllic orange sands and rock formations.

Imagine sharing communion while sailing on the Sea of Galilee; exploring the ruins of Capernaum, where Jesus based his ministry; ascending Mount Nebo where Moses viewed the promised land, and sharing worship, prayer and teaching on the beach where Jesus cooked His disciples breakfast after a long night's fishing. And then there's Petra, the world famous archaeological site in Jordan's southwestern desert. Dating to around 300 B.C., it was the capital of the Nabatean Kingdom. Accessed via a narrow canyon called Al Siq, it contains tombs and temples carved into pink sandstone cliffs. Perhaps its most famous structure is 45m-high Al Khazneh, a temple with an ornate, Greek-style facade and known as the Treasury.

Professional local guides share their wealth of historical and archeological knowledge; Jeff offers teaching as we tour, and Jeff and Kay host the entire experience - one that some travelers have enjoyed so much they have returned to do the same trip a second time!

With excellent hotels, amazing food, and the unforgettable experience of exploring the stunning old city of Jerusalem (with markets where you can haggle for a bargain) this trip will delight and inspire. Come with us!

What others had to say about the tour...

'The memories of this tour are priceless. Jeff brings to life the Bible stories in such a way that one can imagine being there in Bible times.'

'Jeff and Kay kept the momentum of the tour consistent, and the amount of places visited in a very safe and organised fashion is truly remarkable – superb!'

'Our Israel trip was both a spiritual journey and an amazing adventure. Jeff and Kay were great hosts. Our tour guides in Israel and Jordan were knowledgeable and fun.'

'The tour schedule was very manageable and allowed for people to see all the sites, wander alone or just rest. Unforgettable holiday!'

Book your place now and join Jeff and Kay from 9–17 November 2021.

The health and safety of our group members is our number one priority. Our experienced travel agents closely monitor the fast-moving coronavirus situation and are pleased that travel restrictions are being lifted or mitigated in many countries. Our tours strictly adhere to the UK Foreign Office travel advice together with the Israeli Government safety guidelines to ensure all tours operate and conform to any regulations that may be required.

For more information, visit **toursforchristians.com**

In prison again, but no earthquake

Read:
Philippians 1:12–14
Acts 24:1–27

....

FOCUS:

'As a result, it has become clear throughout the whole palace guard and to everyone else that I am in chains for Christ.' (Phil. 1:13)

Let's be reminded of what we read a few days ago – it was in Philippi that Paul and Silas had their late-night worship event interrupted by an earthquake. A miracle happened and prison doors flew open, which ultimately led to their release. Now years have passed. As Paul writes to his friends, and speaks about his chains, we're reminded he's addressing a people who knew well what God had done for him in the past in that jailbreak. But at this point, he has been in prison for two years, and there is no jailbreak in sight.

I can be tempted to want to box God in, and insist that because He intervened in a certain way in my life in the past, He should surely do it again. Or I can have a faith that will trust God as long as He gives me the outcome I want. Obviously, Paul knew God was well able to see him released. But there are no 'why' questions from Paul, just a celebration of grace. He is, however, honest about the pain he feels. He talks of his 'struggle' (some translate this as 'conflict' at the end of the first chapter, verse 30). The Greek word he uses gives us our word 'agony' (*agonia*), and is the same word used for Christ's struggle in the Garden (Luke 22:44).

Later in this chapter, in verse 17, Paul uses the word 'trouble' (*thlipsis*) which means 'inner distress' or 'pain.' In chains, Paul doesn't offer a fake smile, but rather a trusting heart, believing that God was using even his pain in a way that furthered the cause of the gospel.

Prayer: When the answer to my repeated, prayerful request doesn't come as I hope, help me then to firmly trust in You. Amen.

Joyful prayer

Recently I've realised I've been my own worst enemy when it comes to prayer. I've written and spoken a lot about how hard prayer can be, even in these notes, and how I'm not very good at it. My mind wanders into endless distractions, and I fall asleep while trying to focus. It's true that prayer can be difficult, tough work, and I've been happy to share my fragility. But I have come to realise that dwelling on the challenging nature of prayer can rob us of the joy it brings. For Paul, his praying is joyful because it's flavoured with thanksgiving – surely a key to a healthy prayer life. When all we do is ask (though important) we can end up with an unbalanced approach to prayer. Paul's prayer is also joyful because he loves the Philippians so much, as we've seen. And it's joyful because he is able to celebrate his own consistency in prayer – he talks about 'all' his prayers for 'all' the Philippian Christians.

As followers of Jesus, you and I have the incredible privilege of being able to approach the Maker of the Universe with our praises, thankfulness and requests. The writer to the Hebrews celebrates the privilege that is ours; we can 'draw near' with confidence, not because of ceremonies and laws, but because of the total finished victorious work of Christ. We are able to live as humanity was designed to live, in friendship and relationship with the living God. Let's view prayer, challenging though it can be, as a privilege, not a pain.

Prayer: When I need to change my mind and my approach to prayer, renew my thinking, Father. Thank you for the privilege of prayer. Amen.

Read:
Philippians 1:1–6
Hebrews 10:19–25

FOCUS:
'In all my prayers for all of you, I always pray with joy.'
(Phil. 1:4)

the incredible privilege

A prayer for growth

FOCUS:

'And this is my prayer: that your love may abound more and more in knowledge and depth of insight.'
(Phil. 1:9)

When I became a follower of Jesus aged 17, one young man in the youth group really helped me find my feet in the faith. He answered my endless questions and did everything in his power to aid my precarious first steps. All these years later, as far as I know, he is no longer walking with the Lord. As his own youth passed, his heart grew cold, or at least, that's how it seems. An overview of Paul's conversational letter to the church in Philippi reveals he is all about their progress and growth in God. The Lord will complete the good work He began in you, he insists. As we'll see, he wants their love to abound, 'more and more'. And then he speaks of his own desire to continue to grow in his own knowledge of God: 'Not that I have already obtained all this, or have already arrived at my goal, but I press on to take hold of that for which Christ Jesus took hold of me'(Phil. 3:12). He continues; 'Forgetting what is behind and straining toward what is ahead, I press on toward the goal to win the prize for which God has called me heavenward in Christ Jesus' (Phil. 3:13–14). Through all his trials, he is determined to be faithful and move forward.

As I write this today, allow me a moment of self-disclosure. In quarantine because of international travel, I feel weary and disheartened – nothing, I know, compared to what many are facing. But on the tough days, I want to be one who still pursues God, knowing that my feelings are not the barometer of my spirituality.

my feelings are not the barometer of my spirituality

Prayer: Whatever my feelings or circumstances, may I be found faithful, and in pursuit of You, faithful, loving God. Amen.

Solid love – the knowledge of God

This church isn't loving enough. Do something about it!' Angry and frustrated, the woman seemed to think that, as the young pastor of the flock, could magically create a more loving community. She was completely oblivious to her own lack of love for others. As Paul says that he is praying that the love among the Philippians will 'abound more and more' he is echoing a similar hope that he had for the believers in Thessalonica, where he said 'May the Lord make your love increase and overflow for each other and for everyone else, just as ours does for you (1 Thess. 3:12). But commentators note the way he phrases his words means that he is not haranguing them, rather celebrating the beauty of their relationships, and urging them to continue to grow in love. He then uses a phrase that is a little challenging to grasp, as he says that he wants to see their love abound 'more and more in knowledge and depth of insight'.

What is the relationship between love and knowledge? Some commentators think that Paul is pointing them to a love grounded in truth and revelation. Others tell us love is everything, we just need to love people, and to forget about what the Bible says on how we live. But that's a false distinction: God has spoken through His word *because* He loves us. Others see this as pointing us more towards personal experience of knowing God in relationship. Surely both are vital – knowing about God – truth – and knowing God by faith – experience.

Prayer: Father, I want to be grounded in Your word, nourished in Your friendship, rooted in Your love. Amen.

Read:
Philippians 1:9–11
1 Thessalonians 3:6–13

FOCUS:

'And this is my prayer: that your love may abound more and more in knowledge and depth of insight.'
(Phil. 1:9)

Insight and discernment

Read:
Philippians 1:9–11
1 Thessalonians
5:16–24

FOCUS:

'And this is my prayer: that your love may abound more and more in knowledge and depth of insight.'
(Phil. 1:9)

I know, we're camping out on this one phrase that Paul prayed, but this sentence requires careful consideration.

I came across two completely contrasting ministry websites today. One promoted what seemed like mad 'prophetic' words, with a leader summoning angels from the Orient. The other was one of those 'watchman' type sites that focuses on heresy-hunting. Declaring themselves the arbiters of orthodoxy, those who run these websites delight in searching for comments from well-known Christian leaders, often taking them out of context, and then declaring them to be false teachers as a result. My heart sank.

On the one hand, we need to be discerning, and not be suckers for the latest fad going around the church. The word for discernment used here is one taken from the science of metallurgy, where precious metals are tested and proven to be genuine. It has acquired the connotation of 'testing with a view toward approval.' When we think that discernment is a search to enable us to disapprove, we start with the wrong motive. We're told to prove all things, and hold fast to that which is good.

Let's not be foolish. We need to be a people who are insightful. If you'd like a resource to help you dig further the 'Bible Speaks Today' series, published by IVP, is excellent. But as we pursue truth, let's not delight in carping and misquoting either. Neither attitude serves the King or His kingdom. We need to love truth for its own sake.

love truth

Prayer: I want to know what it is to be discerning, but not picky or critical; eager for truth, but not eager to point an accusing finger. Help me, Holy Spirit. Amen.

Read:
Philippians 1:9–11
2 Corinthians 8:1–7

Choosing excellence

I was alarmed when I discovered that our daughter Kelly was planning to run three marathons in three days. Having completed the London and Brighton marathons (forgive me my moment as a proud Dad) she was now embarking on this most demanding event. Her training schedule was extensive, and she often just wanted to take a break and forget the need for a 20-mile run. As it turned out, Covid meant the event was cancelled, but I was impressed by her discipline and determination. Paul often uses athletic metaphors (he does so in Philippians) to illustrate that he wants to choose what is best in his life for the glory of God – athletes train hard to be the very best they can be. There's nothing average or mediocre about Paul's commitment. Sometimes there are moral situations that are not cut and dried, where a compromise is tempting, and we settle for less than the best. When we reach such a junction and have to make a choice, may we follow his example and choose excellence over the average.

To ponder: Is there an area of our lives where we have settled for mediocrity and compromise over excellence and what is best?

Blameless and pure

....

FOCUS:

'so that you may be able to discern what is best and may be pure and blameless for the day of Christ.'
(Phil. 1:10)

It's often been said that the followers of Jesus can put people off Him. We all fail, but when we live in a way that is blatantly hypocritical, it isn't just our reputation that is on the line: it is God's reputation too. As Paul speaks of praying the Philippians will be pure, he uses a word only used twice in the NT – here, and also in 2 Peter 3:1, where it is translated as 'wholesome'. It is *eilikrineis*, which comes from the words for 'sun' and 'to judge', thus indicating purity tested by the light of the sun. And his choice of word translated 'blameless' is interesting. It means we should not behave in a way that causes others to stumble. If our lives are bad news, others will be deterred from believing and accepting the good news.

As the late, great Billy Graham famously remarked, we are the Bibles that the world is reading: they aren't usually reading the actual text. This is also a profoundly biblical truth; we are 'living epistles' or 'letters from Christ', as Paul commented to the believers in Corinth. That statement speaks both of an opportunity and a responsibility. It may be others are quietly watching our lives, wondering if this faith we profess on Sunday is making any difference to the way we act the rest of the week. We aren't called to put on a show, pretending that we don't have issues and struggles, but we are called to live in the power of the Spirit, as godly signposts to others as a result. What difference does our faith make?

we are called to live in the power of the Spirit

Prayer: Live Your life in and through me, Father God, that others might be attracted to You and the life that You offer. Amen.

The fruit of righteousness

'The Bible declares that I am made righteous in Christ' the man said. 'And that means there is nothing else for me to do. It's all covered by the blood of Jesus.' I got the impression he had become careless about sin, which is surely an abuse of grace. But in yet another difficult phrase, Paul is also praying for his friends to be filled with the fruit of righteousness. Most commentators believe he is pointing us back to the truth that in Christ, we have been declared righteous, simply because of the finished work that He has completed. But that work will produce fruit in our lives – what God has done will produce character and grace. Another way of putting this is found in Galatians, where we read about the fruits of the Spirit. Ultimately, it is the life of God at work in our lives that produces fruit, but we have to cooperate with that work, submitting to God, choosing well when temptation comes, walking with God by faith each day. As we choose, He empowers and works. Other commentators point us to the truth that if we walk with the God who is utterly righteous, 'keeping in step with the Spirit', we will display that in our character. We become like the company we keep. James, in his very epistle, talks about the 'harvest of righteousness' (James 3:18)

What we certain is this: walking with the righteous God will result in good fruit in our lives. If the fruit is bad, we have to question the integrity and reality of the walk.

Prayer: Today, my prayer is simple. I want to keep in step with You, that good fruit might come. Amen.

Read:
Philippians 1:9–11
Galatians 5:13–26

FOCUS:
'filled with the fruit of righteousness that comes through Jesus Christ.' (Phil. 1:11)

An eye on the day of the Lord

Read:
Philippians 1:9–11
1 John 3:2–3

FOCUS:

'so that you may be able to discern what is best and may be pure and blameless for the day of Christ.'
(Phil. 1:10)

Imagine what it will be like not to have to struggle with sin or temptation any more. No more hidden motives, no more meandering thoughts to shame us – when we see Jesus, we shall be like Him. So how will that happen? Generally we Christians tend to think that when Christ comes, we will suddenly be transformed to be 'like Christ', as the apostle John promises. And surely that final work will be completed then. But as Paul prays for the Philippians, he reminds them that eternity is in flight now, the academy of transformation is in session, and our growth and maturity are aiming for that final day of the Lord. And John in his writing assures us we will be like Christ on that great day, and then affirms that those with this hope purify themselves.

Here I confess that, much of the time, I don't live with a sense of the coming of Jesus. The early Christians, living so close to death, had a far greater perspective on life and death. For us, the here and now is very much in focus, and is our major preoccupation. And living in the light of eternity has been made even more difficult by foolish teaching and speculation about the Second Coming. Those scriptures that talk about Jesus coming again have been so misused, many of us who preach and teach are easily tempted to neglect or even ignore them. Today, in cooperation with the Holy Spirit, I want to grow to be a little more like Jesus, because tomorrow or at some time in the future, His great day will come.

Prayer: I will be like You, Jesus. May that transforming work continue in me today and I choose purity and righteousness. Amen.

All for God's glory

Read:
Philippians 1:9–11
John 15:1–8

FOCUS:
'filled with the fruit of righteousness that comes through Jesus Christ—to the glory and praise of God' (Phil. 1:11)

'You're a what?' It was a very long flight, and the chap sitting next to me seemed very keen to talk. All was going rather well until he asked me what my work was. Usually I respond to questions about my occupation by talking about writing and speaking, rather than jumping into the 'I'm a Christian minister' conversation, which has been known to swiftly shut down any further dialogue. But on this occasion, I jumped right into the pastoral side of my work. Popping another peanut into his mouth, his eyes grew wide. He was incredulous that I would spend my life as a Christian leader. 'That religious stuff... it's all so very... irrelevant', he muttered. And that's the tragedy of it, that some have rejected God, not because He is too demanding, but because the notion of Him seems antiquated, dull, other-worldly. The image of the Church is often that we are strange and out of touch. When we hear Paul praying for his friends to be enabled to live a life for God's glory and praise, our motives are challenged. Our task is to live beautifully, not for self-promotion but, as we saw earlier, to point people to the God who is the author of that beauty, and also to show how utterly relevant He is. The word 'glory' in translated by some commentators to mean 'important'. Walking with Jesus, in a sense, is not an optional extra, but a vital call to live as we have been designed to live. When we live well, we make God relevant, and show the importance of knowing Him.

Prayer: May Your people glorify You today, ever-living, ever-loving Father. Amen.

live as we have been designed to live

Looking for summer reading?
We've got it covered...

Now is the perfect time to explore these books...

Specks and Planks: Stories of Hope, Humility and Humanity

Jeff Lucas

Staying in the Boat: And Other Things I Wish I'd Known

Jeff Lucas

The Dog Who Thought His Name Was No

Judy Moore

Unwavering: The Power of Choice (An Inspiring Women Book)

Jen Baker

**Unshakeable Confidence
(An Inspiring Women Book)**

Jen Baker

Life Together: The Family Devotional

Steve and Bekah Legg

**Cold Cups of Tea and Hiding in the Loo:
An Honest Look at Parenting**

Annie Wilmot

The Activity Bible (Ages 4–7)

The Activity Bible (Ages 7–11)

To order these titles and dive into your next great read, visit
waverleyabbeyresources.org

Prayer for the Colossian Christians

Read:
Colossians 2:6–8
1 Timothy 6:20–21

FOCUS:

'See to it that no one takes you captive through hollow and deceptive philosophy, which depends on human tradition and the elemental spiritual forces of this world rather than on Christ.' (Col. 2:8)

As we turn now to a prayer Paul prayed for the church in Colossae, we see the Church has been battling to guard the purity of the gospel since it bega. A 'faith in Jesus is not enough' idea was circulating in a number of churches in that area, suggesting one had to have 'secret knowledge' (Gnosticism) in order to be saved. The apostle Paul, now in prison, wasn't the founder of these congregations, but had been asked t help by Epaphras, the man who was. Hence this letter.

It's unclear whether these errors were being sprea by people in the congregations, or had been importec by visiting speakers, but whatever their source, the church was being slowly moved away from the simplicity of the gospel, lured by the promise of an apparent 'deeper' spiritual life. False teaching always comes with the promise that those who follow it will b more authentic and substantial in their faith, and any who challenge it are deemed to be unspiritual.

Living in the digital age as we do, with easy access to billions of words, the potential for unhelpful teaching is greater than ever. I don't want to suggest that we create a culture of suspicion, where everyone is assumed to be wrong unless we have checked them out and declared them right and orthodox. We have already seen some Christians and sections of the church taking that approach. But we do have a responsibility to think through and reflect biblically o what we are taught, whatever its source.

Prayer: In pursuing depth in my faith, save me from distraction or error, Father. Amen.

Read:
Colossians 1:1–8
John 3:16

Widening prayer's circle

The horizon of my praying often seems to shrink. Preoccupied by my own concerns, questions, requests, I pray for those closest to me and, by the time that's done, I'm out of energy. But Paul prays for a people he has never met. He didn't plant the church in Colossae, and he has never visited it. Epaphras, one of his own sons in the faith, had planted the church, so perhaps he felt an affinity with his spiritual 'grandchildren'. Nevertheless his habit of praying for them challenges us to make sure that the focus of our prayers doesn't get narrowed. Why not take a few simple steps to widen your own horizon of prayer? When you hear a country mentioned on the news, pray for that nation and especially the believers in it. Adopt a missionary. Get news from an agency which supports and shares news of the persecuted church. Let's enlarge the focus of our prayers beyond us, where we live and those whom we know. God loves the world. As we pray broadly, we show our love for it too.

ponder: What other habits could you embrace to make sure that you pray widely?

God loves the world

Thankful for God's people

Read:
Colossians 1:3–8
Romans 1:1–8

FOCUS:

'We always thank God, the Father of our Lord Jesus Christ, when we pray for you.' (Col. 1:3)

During the Covid crisis, many churches shone wonderfully as they helped coordinate community responses to the struggles. Local teams wore themselves out producing online resources. I witnessed a wonderful moment just before the lockdown. The foodbank facility based in C3 church in Cambridge was working overtime to help, and I watched as a long line formed to collect vital supplies. One lady, her eyes brimming with tears, took her food box and smiled, 'You're just wonderful, you people. Thank you so much for all that you're doing to help us. You're lifesavers.' I felt humbled and thankful to be part of God's Church.

We saw earlier that when Paul prayed for the churches, he did so with thanksgiving, a detail that we could so easily miss. Fully aware of the challenges and often frustrated by unkind words directed at him, Paul celebrated his relationships with thankfulness to God. That provokes me to be more focused on thankfulness generally, and to embrace a discipline of being thankful that I am part of a wonderful, dynamic, local church. It far from perfect (not least because I am part of it), but it truly is a privilege to belong, to have come out of the chill of aloneness and be part of the Christian family. We can take the warmth of togetherness for granted. Be thankful for fellowship today. Spend some time giving thanks to the Lord for some specific people in your church environment, and ask God to encourage them. Or why not encourage them yourself?

Prayer: I am called into a family, with all the privileges and challenges that follow. Thank You for making me part of Your people, Lord. Amen.

Repeated prayer

When our children ask for something – chocolate, a new toy, another piece of cake, and we have to refuse them – we don't usually encourage them to keep on asking. Nagging persistence is not naturally celebrated, and we expect them to take no for an answer. But when it comes to prayer, God takes a different view, and encourages us to bring our requests to Him repeatedly, as the parable of the importunate or persistent widow (Luke 18:1–8) shows very clearly. Jesus taught that we 'should always pray and not give up'.

Paul obviously understood that principle, letting the Colossians know he had 'not stopped' praying for them, a comment that he makes elsewhere – the church in Rome also received the assurance of Paul's ongoing prayers. And young Timothy was given similar reassurance by Paul: 'I thank God, whom I serve, as my ancestors did, with a clear conscience, as night and day I constantly remember you in my prayers (2 Tim. 1:3). This doesn't mean that Paul was engaged in a mystical state of constant prayer, but instead was diligent and disciplined in repeating his intercessions for others.

Here I come to another moment of confession. Over four decades of ministry, I have not taken sufficient time to ask for the consistent prayerful support of others. And that suggests that I have underestimated the significance and power of prayer. So forgive me for asking, but may I ask for your prayers today. I, in turn, will pray for all who join me for *Life Every Day*.

Prayer: I want to be consistent and persistent in prayer, Lord. Teach me how to pray like that. Amen.

Read:
Colossians 1:9
Romans 1:8–10

FOCUS:
'For this reason, since the day we heard about you, we have not stopped praying for you.' (Col. 1:9)

bring our
requests
to Him
repeatedly

Knowing God's will

Read:
Colossians 1:9–12
Ephesians 5:17

FOCUS:

'We continually ask God to fill you with the knowledge of his will.' (Col. 1:9)

Regular readers of *Life Every Day* will perhaps recall some of my early struggles with knowing the will of God. Plagued with fear that I might make a wrong turn, I was terrified of living a 'second best' life, and fretted endlessly over even minor decisions. Abandoning that paranoia some years ago, I fear I went to the other extreme, and at times rushed into projects without taking time to pause and submit my plans to God, with some inevitably bad results. As Paul prays for the Colossians, he wants them to know what God wants for them and then live in alignment with His purpose for them. While I no longer believe that God has an opinion or preference about every single detail of my life, I remain convinced He has headline objectives for me, a broad mission in life that I am appointed to embrace and fulfil. But this is not limited to the specific directions of our lives, which God may give guidance on. In many cases, God's will has already been revealed. It is God's will that we be sanctified, set apart for Him and growing in His likeness (1 Thess. 4:3). We also know that God wills that we rejoice, pray continually, and give thanks (1 Thess. 5:16–18). We don't have to ask God if He wants us to become more like Jesus every day.

There is divine purpose in you being alive today. Just as Paul prayed for his friends that they might know and live in that purpose, may you know the joy that comes when we live in alignment with what God wants for us.

Prayer: I pray for those that I love, that not only will they be blessed, but that they will know and live in Your will and purposes for their lives, Father. Amen.

Spirit-fuelled wisdom and understanding

Read:
Colossians 1:9–12
Ephesians 1:17

FOCUS:
'We continually ask God to fill you with the knowledge of his will through all the wisdom and understanding that the Spirit gives.'
(Col. 1:9)

One of the great challenges for the Church today is the lack of basic biblical knowledge among believers. We're living in an ethical maze, where many foundational truths about how we should live are being questioned. When I hear Christians debate controversial issues, they often mention love and human rights – both vital components of any difficult conversation. But, without sounding too much like an old chap blustering on about the younger generation, I'm concerned that often believers don't refer to biblical truths. People don't know their Bibles, and they seem to be indifferent to their lack of knowledge. When we look around the world and see the price the persecuted church pays because of their love of Scripture, as we have seen, we should be motivated again to immerse ourselves in biblical truth.

In praying for the Colossians, Paul takes them beyond mere intellectual knowledge. In Paul's day, Jews believed they would know God's will by studying God's law. But Paul wants the Colossians to know that another dynamic helper is involved in the process: the Holy Spirit, who comes alongside us and fills us so that we experience a supernatural dynamic as we pursue God's purposes.

I've certainly experienced that Word and Spirit coalition in my own life, feeling at times that I was being led on a trail of discovery to enable me to make a good choice. Today, read and reflect on Scripture, and ask the Holy Spirit to fill you and help you as you do so.

Prayer: Spirit of Truth, fill me, enlighten me, direct me, enlarge my understanding of You. Amen.

read and reflect on Scripture

Walk worthy

Read:
Colossians 1:9–12
1 Thessalonians
2:1–12

....

FOCUS:

*'so that you may live
a life worthy of the
Lord.' (Col. 1:10)*

We're returning to a theme we touched on earlier – living in a way that points to God. It's always a tragedy when a high-profile Christian leader gets entangled in moral scandal. Their ministry usually ends, their families are hurt, and those who trusted them in the church feel devastated. How could they teach one thing and live a totally contradictory lifestyle? But there is another devastating result of their so-called 'falls' (I hesitate to use the word 'fall' because most of the time these sad episodes come from a gradual slide). The reputation of the Church – and the God of the Church – is damaged, as we have seen already. So when a leader consistently lives in a way that brings discredit, action must be taken. How we live affects those we represent. Let's be reminded again that we represent Jesus. Our lives are not our own, and what we do profoundly affects the way others look at the God we profess to serve.

Paul calls the Colossians to live a life 'worthy of the Lord'. Writing to the Ephesians, he exhorts them to 'live a life worthy of the calling you have received (Eph. 4:1). A similar call is given to the Thessalonians. For good or ill, those around us will make judgments about God and the gospel based on what they see in our lives. If we're drifting into 'unworthy' lifestyles, we should remember that, while we tell ourselves we're not hurting anyone, we may well be harming the reputation of God Himself.

Prayer: I bear Your name, Jesus. By grace, may I walk worthily. Amen.

we represent
Jesus

Read:
Colossians 1:9–12
2 Corinthians 5:1–10

Pleasing God

My memories of my grandfathers are limited. My maternal grandfather was a decorated war hero, having served with distinction in the First World War. A gentle, kindly man, he gave me my love of words, reading stories to me for hours. He lived with our family, and so I saw him close up. My maternal step-grandfather was the opposite. A hard, angry man, I can't remember a moment of tenderness from him. Whatever I did as a child, he wasn't pleased. If I sat on the floor, he told me to get up and find a chair, and vice versa. His face fell naturally into a disapproving scowl.

Many of us think of God as more like the latter than the former, but Paul prays the Colossians (and we) might know how we can 'please the Lord in every way'. We will consider that in more detail, but for now, let's know we can live in a way that brings a smile to His face and great joy to His heart. Pleasing God was Paul's great ambition. We won't reach perfection this side of eternity, but we can please Him today.

To ponder: Do you find it easy to think of being able to please God?

Visit **waverleyabbey
resources.org
/podcast** to listen
to a podcast

Fruit again

Read:
Colossians 1:9–12
Ephesians 2:1–10

....

FOCUS:

'bearing fruit in every good work' (Col. 1:10)

We're back to fruitfulness again, which bring a slight pang, because I'm not a gardener. On the contrary, most things that I plant wither and die (apart from the jasmine I mentioned earlier). Sent to do a little weed clearing, I tend to water the weeds and dig up the plants. In confronting the false teachers in Colossae who boasted of great revelations, Paul exposes the reality: for all their talk, their deep insights had not led to anything useful or practical. Bad or false teaching never does. Now Paul prays the believers in the city will be fruitful. He is not looking for a claim of deeper knowledge, but the beauty of 'every good work'. The idea that Christians will be people of good works is central in all of Paul's writings. He also speaks of good works in Romans 13:3; 2 Corinthians 9:8; Galatians 6:10 and Titus 1:16.

Let's affirm this truth, because sometimes Paul is presented in opposition to James. Paul does focus on justification by faith, whereas James looks for good works that follow true faith. But again, so does Paul. We are not saved *by* our works, but we are saved *for* good works as part of God's eternal plan.

It was through 'good works' that the Early Church made such an impact. As they cared for the sick and dying in pandemics, (and not just their own people) and often at great personal risk, the ancient world saw a transformed, fruitful people, and an entirely new and different attitude. The opportunity and challenge are the same today.

Prayer: I am saved by Your work, and called to do good work as a result. Use my life today, spend me, Father. Amen.

The opportunity and challenge are the same today.

God's Playlist

The Psalms introduce us to the inner thoughts, beliefs, praises and fears of those who wrote them, in particular King David, who was responsible for at least 73 of them. In his writing, we find our own lives: and we also learn more about, and see more clearly, the God he served, and we serve as well. Join Jeff Lucas for a careful introduction to this very important Bible book, one that celebrates humanity in all its aspects, as well as the Creator of that humanity.

Also available as eBook/eSubscription

Growing in the knowledge of God

Read:
Colossians 1:9–12
2 Peter 1:1–2

....

FOCUS:

'growing in the knowledge of God'
(Col. 1:10)

Regular *Life Every Day* readers will know that I've described how 'testimony times' were a regular feature of some Christian gatherings years ago. We'd get together, share what God had done for us recently, or perhaps recount the story of how we came to faith. One of the phrases often used in those wonderful occasions was, 'I came to know the Lord.' Strictly speaking, that's a biblical statement. Peter writes in his second epistle about how we know the Lord. But in his prayer for the Colossians, Paul makes it clear that knowing God is also a progressive experience, just as knowledge of a person is gradual in any relationship. One day we will have 'full' knowledge (1 Cor. 13:12), but in the meantime, we're called to mature in our understanding of His character, learn from our interaction with Him, glean insights from what we experience in His dealings with us. Remember there were false teachers in the church in Colossae who were touting so-called deeper teaching that was worthless: Paul in his prayer points us to the truth that what really matters is not what you know, but who you know. Knowing God is to be our primary pursuit. Once again, we're reminded of Paul's passionate affirmation to the Philippians. He had come to know the Lord on the Damascus road when he had an incredible experience of Jesus and heard His audible voice. But yesterday's experience was not enough. He was hungry, determined to know God more. May we share his appetite.

Prayer: I want to know You more, Jesus. Reveal Yourself to me; show me Your ways; show me Yourself. Amen.

Strengthened with mighty power

As we hear Paul praying that the Colossians would be 'strengthened with all power' we're reminded of his words to the Philippians: 'I can do all this through him who gives me strength'. Often this is translated as 'I can do all things through him' – giving the impression that we can do *anything* through God's power. I've sometimes questioned someone's ability in a particular area, and they've responded, 'But I can do all things.' That's a misunderstanding. God's power is given to enable us to fulfil God's purposes. Obviously, we all have limitations. I can't fly to the moon, (without the assistance of a rocket) give birth to twins, or play the bassoon (without practice). And there are limits to my gifts and calling, which is why I gave up worship leading decades ago, much to the relief of all who had endured my self-perceived gift at that time.

All that said, power is available, and to emphasise the point, Paul prays they will experience God's power, according to His glorious might'. Elsewhere, writing to the Ephesians, Paul uses the example of God raising Jesus from the dead as the supreme example of His staggering power, and reminds us, this very same power is at work in us. Next time we're tempted to mutter 'I'm only human', let's remember nothing could be farther from the truth. The Christian is not just a person turned religious; the Christian is a new creation, part of a whole new species of humanity, created in Christ, empowered by His Spirit.

Prayer: I am a new creation in You, Jesus. Help me to live for the good of that reality today. Amen.

Read:
Colossians 1:9–12
Philippians 4:13

FOCUS:
'being strengthened with all power according to his glorious might.'
(Col. 1:11).

the Christian is a new creation

Endurance

Read:
Colossians 1:9–12
**2 Corinthians
11:22–33**

....

FOCUS:

*'so that you may
have great
endurance.' (Col. 1:11)*

We live in a culture obsessed with the lives of celebrities. Super-fast communications mean that they can post comments, photos and videos of their exploits and instantly connect with millions. We seem enthralled by the lives of the rich, the famous, the beautiful. But surely God has a different way of measuring heroic behaviour, which has absolutely nothing to do with fame, finance, looks or talent. Over my years in ministry I have met countless heroes, and most have never stood on a public platform. They are the courageous souls who cling fast to faith, even though at times they feel assailed by doubt and uncertainty; they are the prayer warriors who battle physical pain daily but still pray for the healing of others; they are the solitary souls who, whenever there's a task to be done in the church community, show up, do it, and don't get bitter. They keep going, much of the time enduring life rather than enjoying it because of the harsh circumstances they're in.

In praying for the Colossians to be able to endure, Paul had plenty of experience. His words to the Corinthians powerfully outline the trials he'd walked through, which were many, extended and painful. Just one of the harrowing episodes that he suffered might have tempted us to give up and throw in the towel on faith. But knowing what he knew, and who he knew, kept Paul going. If you are one of those enduring heroes today, may You know God's strength and smile

Prayer: I pray today for those who endure life rather than enjoying it. Be their portion, their source, their comfort today, Lord. Amen.

atience

⌐he church leader sighed. He'd just been through
a bruising annual church meeting where a few
cal congregants had savagely attacked him. His
rmons weren't deep enough, his pastoral care was
different, and his leadership was weak. I know the
an well, and none of these accusations are true. He
a scholar and a fine communicator; his ministry has
en successful because he is a proactive, strategic
ader; and he deeply cares for the people of his
urch and the wider community.

⌐he pastor looked down, defeat written all over his
ce. 'I've been doing this Christian leadership thing
r four decades', he lamented. 'I'm not sure how much
re I can take. I love Jesus, but His people sometimes
ve me crazy.'

Perhaps we've all been there. Our experience of
cal church can be disappointing, dull, even bruising.
times we're tempted to abandon the whole church
perience altogether. But as Paul adds the word
tience' to his prayers, the context of the word
usually in relationships. In the third chapter of
lossians, Paul returns again to patience and calls the
lossians to bear with each other (Col. 3:12–13). Again,
the Ephesians he writes: 'Be completely humble and
ntle; be patient, bearing with one another in love' (Eph.
). Being part of the family of God is both a privilege
d requires patience. And who knows – perhaps
meone is reading these notes and thinking ruefully
out needing to be patient with you – or me – right now!

ayer: Lord, grant me patience in fellowship, and grant
se I'm in fellowship with patience with me. Amen.

Read:
Colossians 1:9–12
Ephesians 4:2

FOCUS:
'so that you may
have great
endurance and
patience.' (Col. 1:11).

bear with
each other

Weekend

Thankfulness again

As I write this, my family members and friends in America are celebrating Thanksgiving – one of my favourite times of the year. I love Christmas, but so enjoy the simple beauty of Thanksgiving, where people gather to be grateful, without all the commercialism and pressure of Christmas. But for Paul, thankfulness was a daily discipline. Frequently he mingles his prayers with declarations of gratitude – and remember, he prayed this prayer while under house arrest – an extended lockdown, if you will. I hesitate to say this because I know some readers of *Life Every Day* face hugely challenging circumstances, but I believe there are always reasons to be thankful, whatever our current difficulties. For Paul, (and Peter in his epistle) thanksgiving was FOCUS: ed not on circumstances, but rather on what God had done in Christ – the giving of blessings or inheritance, the ability to belong among the holy people of God, the wonder of being in light rather than darkness. Today, give thanks.

To ponder: Biblical thanksgiving seems to focus more on what God has done rather than our current circumstances. Do we need to adjust what we're thankful for?

iving in what God has said

lipping through the pages of a study book recently,
I discovered some notes that I had scribbled in it.
r some reason I'd decided to note something God
s clearly spoken to me back then. A journal would be
tter, but I was glad to be reminded of some promises
d had made, promises that have come to pass. I was
minded – I am living in the calling of God. As Paul
ntinues to celebrate the work of Christ, enabling
to be kingdom people, redeemed and forgiven, he
noes very closely what Jesus said to him years earlier
the Damascus Road – the command to 'to open their
es and turn them from darkness to light, and from
e power of Satan to God, so that they may receive
giveness of sins and a place among those who are
nctified by faith in me'. Notice the parallel themes
tween that calling and Paul's words to the Colossians.
Even though that command had been given years
rlier, Paul was still living closely to it.

As we begin to draw our reflections on some of
ul's words to a close, perhaps it would be good to
use and consider any specific directions, promises
commands that we feel God has given us in our
urneys of faith. Are His purposes for us still our
mary purpose? Writing to Timothy, Paul was able to
y that he was finishing well: 'I have fought the good
ht, I have finished the race, I have kept the faith'
Tim. 4:7). As we live in alignment to God's purposes
us, we will be able to say the same.

yer: I want to do Your will, live in Your calling and
rpose for me, all the days of my life, faithful God.
en.

Read:
Colossians 1:13
Acts 26:1–18

FOCUS:

'For he has rescued
us from the
dominion of
darkness and
brought us into the
kingdom of the Son
he loves, in whom
we have redemption,
the forgiveness of
sins.' (Col. 1:13)

alignment
to God's
purposes
for us

A man of action and prayer

Read:
Colossians 4:2–6
Mark 1:35–37

....

FOCUS:
*'Devote yourselves to
prayer, being
watchful and
thankful.' (Col. 4:2)*

As we end our time with Paul and some of his prayers, we hear him calling the Colossians to prayerful watchfulness. This was an exhortation to careful, steady faith for the long haul. As a church planter, Paul achieved so much with his tireless travels, never thwarted by pressure or persecution. His pastoral care and scholarly writing gave us the great doctrines of the faith, and he wrote a third of the New Testament. But Paul was no mere activist, busy and hurried for the kingdom. His acts of service and ministry were rooted in a deep, rich spirituality. His passion to make Christ known flowed, not just from one divine encounter, but a daily, depending knowledge of Jesus. Having spent himself in prayer, he called the Colossians – and us – to live the same way.

We follow the Jesus who would often steal away to spend time with the Father. Before making major decisions, He prioritised that relationship. Shortly after becoming a Christian, I was influenced by teaching that undermined the need for the daily 'quiet time'. For some, the practice of daily prayerful retreat had become a legalistic snare, and they needed to know God's love was not dependent on them spending a certain amount of time in prayer each day. But looking back, we lost something vital and precious, a true source of life: solitude, reflection, prayerful retreat. For Paul, and for Jesus, disciplined prayer was vital. May we follow in their footsteps. And thanks for joining me.

solitude,
reflection,
prayerful
retreat

Prayer: I will seek Your face, Lord. Teach me afresh how to pray. Amen.

rder form

Easy Ways To Order

Visit our online store at **waverleyabbeyresources.org/store**

Send this form together with your payment to: **Waverley Abbey Resources, Waverley Abbey House, Waverley Lane, Farnham, Surrey GU9 8EP**

Phone in your credit card order: **01252 784700** (Mon–Fri, 9.30am – 4.30pm)

Visit a Christian bookshop

For Australia and New Zealand visit KI Entertainment **kigifts.com.au**

a list of our National Distributors, who supply countries outside the UK, visit waverleyabbeyresources.org/distributors

our Details (required for orders and donations)

ull Name:	CWR ID No. (if known):
ome Address:	
	Postcode:
elephone No. (for queries):	Email:

ublications

TITLE	QTY	PRICE	TOTAL
		Total Publications	

K P&P: up to £24.99 = **£2.99**; £25.00 and over = **FREE**

sewhere P&P: up to £10 = **£4.95**; £10.01 – £50 = **£6.95**; £50.01 – £99.99 = **£10**; £100 and over = **£30**

tal Publications and P&P (please allow 14 days for delivery) **A**

ubscriptions* (non direct debit)

	QTY	PRICE (including P&P)			TOTAL
		UK	Europe	Elsewhere Please contact nearest National Distributor or CWR direct	
'e Every Day (Jeff Lucas) (1yr, 6 issues)		£17.95	£22.50		
tal Subscriptions (subscription prices already include postage and packing)				**B**	

v use this section for subscriptions paid for by credit/debit card or cheque. For Direct Debit subscriptions see overleaf.

WR adult Bible reading notes are also available in single issue **ebook** and **email subscription** format. waverleyabbeyresources.org for further information.

se circle which issue you would like your subscription to commence from:

FEB MAR/APR MAY/JUN JUL/AUG SEP/OCT NOV/DEC

Continued overleaf >>

How would you like to hear from us? We would love to keep you up to date on all aspects of the CWR try, including; new publications, events & courses as well as how you can support us.

DO want to hear from us on email, please tick here [ ]

DO NOT want us to contact you by post, please tick here [ ]

update your preferences at any time by contacting our customer services team on 01252 784 700. You can view our privacy policy online at waverleyabbeyresources.org

Payment Details

☐ I enclose a cheque/PO made payable to CWR for the amount of: £ _____

☐ Please charge my credit/debit card.

Cardholder's Name (in BLOCK CAPITALS) _____

Card No. ☐☐☐☐ ☐☐☐☐ ☐☐☐☐ ☐☐☐☐

Expires End ☐☐ ☐☐   Security Code ☐☐☐

Gift to CWR   ☐ Please send me an acknowledgement of my gift   **C** ☐

Gift Aid (your home address required, see overleaf)

giftaid it I am a UK taxpayer and want CWR to reclaim the tax on all my donations for the four years prior to this **and on** all donations I make from the date of this Gift Aid declaration until further notice.*

Taxpayer's Full Name (in BLOCK CAPITALS) _____

Signature _____ **Date** _____

*I am a UK taxpayer and understand that if I pay less Income Tax and/or Capital Gains Tax than the amount of Gift Aid claimed on all my donations in th year it is my responsibility to pay any difference.

GRAND TOTAL (Total of A, B & C) ☐

Subscriptions by Direct Debit (UK bank account holders only)

One-year subscriptions (6 issues a year) cost £17.95 and include UK delivery. Please tick relevant boxes and fill in the form below.

☐ *Life Every Day* (Jeff Lucas)

Issue to commence from

☐ Jan/Feb   ☐ Mar/Apr   ☐ May/Jun   ☐ Jul/Aug   ☐ Sep/Oct   ☐ Nov/Dec

CWR Instruction to your Bank or Building Society to pay by Direct Debit

DIRE **Deb**

Please fill in the form and send to: CWR, Waverley Abbey House, Waverley Lane, Farnham, Surrey GU9 8EP

Name and full postal address of your Bank or Building Society

To: The Manager _____ Bank/Building Society

Address _____

_____

_____

Postcode _____

Name(s) of Account Holder(s)

_____

Branch Sort Code

☐☐ ☐☐ ☐☐

Bank/Building Society Account Number

☐☐☐☐☐☐☐☐

Originator's Identification Number

4	2	0	4	8	7

Reference

☐☐☐☐☐☐☐☐☐☐☐☐☐

Instruction to your Bank or Building Society

Please pay CWR Direct Debits from the account detailed in this Ir subject to the safeguards assured by the Direct Debit Guarantee. I understand that this Instruction may remain with CWR and, if so will be passed electronically to my Bank/Building Society.

Signature(s)

_____

Date

_____

Banks and Building Societies may not accept Direct Debit Instructions for some types of account